DIY Survival:

Deadly Projects for Self-Defense

Table of Contents

Introduction

Welcome to DIY Survival Projects: Deadly Defenses, a DIY book about prepping your home with a deadly defense that can kill your enemies or harm them enough to where you can protect your family. As we come nearer and nearer to nasty times and more of us become dependent on nature rather than the government, having natural defenses built up in-house goes a long way to making sure we can sleep soundly at night. This book is not only built to help you identify how you can build your traps effectively and for specific purposes but also shows you a wide range of different traps you can make yourself. Let's begin.

Chapter 1 – The Purpose of Deadly Defense

As with all my books, I prefer to inform people about what they're trying to build rather than what they think this book is all about right from the start. The title of this book may suggest that the book is all about ways to kill your opponents if you get into a situation where you need to defend your house. While there may be a few of those projects in here, a good portion of these projects are just early warning systems or built to slow down the opponent so let's go over why these are considered deadly defenses.

Early Detection

Early detection is one of the best possible stances you could have because not only does it wake you up whenever you're completely unaware of something that may be happening outside of your perimeter but it also allows you to get prepared for what you need to do. Instead of some person or thing showing up unannounced, an early detection system allows you to prepare for an opponent before they ever get the chance to surprise you. The reason why this is called a deadly defense is because it is deadly for your opponent in the fact that you can ready your crossbows, your shotguns, or any other weapons you have the second the alarm goes off so that you can defend your house.

Surprise Attack

A surprise attack is a little bit different than an early detection method because instead of just letting you know someone is there, you get to find out that he, she or it is there because they will usually yell at the same time that they are attacked. These type of attacks are meant to do moderate to severe damage to your opponent before they ever get to your doorstep and also be utilized as a way for you to detect them inside of your perimeter earlier than you would have before. A lot of people love surprise attack methods and will generally just make books based around surprise attacks but the problem with most surprise attacks is that they tend to only work once and if they didn't even work then they failed at what they're supposed to do and you are now unprepared. This is the reason why you want surprise attacks to come in small packages because you can build more than one of them so that if one fails another might not.

Physical Damage

The last one is to just do physical damage and these are really meant to either defend your home or defend you while you run away in your home or away from your home. These are meant to slow down your opponent more than anything else and while some of them may kill your opponent, the entire purpose of them is to cause physical damage and to slow them down.

These are the principles behind deadly defenses and as you can see they're not all meant to directly kill your opponents but rather help you help yourself. While a good portion of these will probably kill your opponent, you still need to be able to rely on yourself to handle the bulk of the damage that you need to do to the enemy.

Chapter 1 – Early Detection

Sounding The Alarm

Items

- Airhorn

- Tripwire

- Propped Heavy Object

Instructions

The first thing that you want to do whenever you're trying to set up your house for a defense is you want an early detection system and pretty much anything with an air horn will do the trick. In this one, we're actually using the benefit of gravity on our side because if you press down on the air horn just a little bit then the air horn will go off. For this one, all you need to do is lay the air horn on the ground preferably in a dug out hole so that your opponent cannot see it, and then you need to hold a heavy object above the air horn. This heavy object should be propped up by a stick or some other item that can easily be pulled up or out. The item that you'll be pulling out will be tied to a tripwire so that you can tie that tripwire to something that's solidly in the ground either very close by or very far away but the idea is that you want the area between the heavy object and the base of the tripwire to be at least an inch or two off the ground. It's also ideal to hide this in a location where there's a lot of grass because you don't exactly want your opponent to easily notice the tripwire. What will happen is that the opponent will push on the tripwire and the tripwire will pull the support out and, usually, this will additionally trip the opponent and then the heavy object will fall on the air horn and the air horn will be pushed, which sounds the alarm.

Sonic Alarm

Items

- Sound Grenade or Alarm

- Tripwire

- A Cloth The Same Color As Where You Are Putting It

Instructions

Perhaps one of the easiest methods of early detection that does rely on current factories is the Sonic grenade or the Sonic alarm that you can make with a simple tripwire or fishing wire but essentially you just want some type of wire that won't break whenever it's been stepped on or cold to be attached to the sound grenade. Once you have set up the wire where you want it to be and the sound grenade is in a good acoustic place like a hole that will amplify the noise that is heard, you want to select a piece of cloth that is very similar to the surrounding area of the tripwire as well as the sound grenade. First, you want to place this cloth on it and it should not be heavy enough to weigh down the wire to the point where it pulls the pin from the Sonic grenade but it should also be good enough to blend in with some of its environment in that area. Ideally, you want the tripwire to be anywhere from two to three inches above the ground so that the foot can make it underneath the wire as they are walking forward. To add to this, if you are placing this type of early detection system out in the yard then you can also cover these bits of cloth with a bit of mud so that it is even further disguised and they have a harder time detecting where it is especially since the most common time that you're going to be attacked is during the night as it is much easier for them to get in the house unnoticed. While some people may be guarding the house at night, everyone has to sleep eventually and no one wants somebody to be asleep during the day just so that they can guard during the night.

Chapter 2 – Wire Traps

Electric Fence

Items

- Tripwire

- Electric Source

Instructions

Making an electric fence is actually really easy because all you need is a wire and an electrical source along with a ton of space. An electric wire is really just a completed circuit that is not protected. A case in point is whenever you're dealing with a light bulb and you have to plug the light bulb in by turning it into the socket. The light bulb is just a thin strip of wire inside of a closed environment that has a specific type of gas that allows it to be more luminescent than before. On the other hand, an electric fence is a wire that's been wrapped around the positive part of an electrical source and then brought down and around the area, you want to protect before coming back to the electrical source to be wrapped around the negative side. What happens is that the electrons pass from the electrical source through the wire, around the wire, and finally back into the power source. If there is nothing protecting the wire then it will zap anything it touches.

Hallway Tripper

Items

- Tripwire

- A Drill

- A Hallway

Instructions

This is perhaps the easiest version of home defense because you can either set it up so that you can pull on the wire so that an unexpected tripping wire comes out from the side of a wall or you can set it up to trip anyone who's walking down the hall while you're trying to sleep. Essentially, all you want to do is drill a hole in either one or both sides of the wall so that you can feed the tripwire through the hole. Now the reason why I say you could do one or both sides because if you have the style of house where your whole hallway is one part wall and one part stair railing then you could drill a hole in the wall and tie the tripwire to the stairwell railing. So once you have the tripwire through the hole then all you need to do is tie it to something that you can pull on and then the other side needs to be tied to something that will permanently stay in place or be pulled into a position where it can provide resistance to lift the tripwire off the ground by around 2 to 3 inches. You want this much room because the average foot is around two to three inches tall.

Swinging Weapon

Items

- Tripwire

- Two Blocks of Wood

- A Spear or Weapon with heavy mass to it

- Five Nails

Instructions

The swinging spears are a little bit different than the hallway tripper because you need to build it a little bit differently. Essentially, you put two blocks of wood on the sides of the wall near the ceiling and then nail those blocks of wood in with one of those nails partially sticking out so that you can tie the tripwire to it before nailing it in further. You will want to make sure that the tripwire has at least a little bit of freedom to swing back and forth because you're going to be using this to propel your spear forward. Once those are nailed in you now need to attach the tripwire to a spear object. Now depending on the spear, you may actually have the ability to just hang the spear up but most of the time you will want to just place the tripwire in the middle of the spear so that it can be rocked forward and the weight of the spear can be what's used to penetrate the skin. Likewise, you can also attach something else beyond the spear like a medicine ball so that it can be supported until you need to use it and then the medicine ball will drop down and give your opponent a good thrashing. This is a trap that you can set up with other traps such as the hallway tripper because then it does two things at once. For instance, if you have the wire set up so that the wire is pulled out of its place so that it flies forward at the same time as the hallway tripper activates then you can easily watch your opponent not only trip but also fall face-first into your other trap.

Spear Trap

Items

- Tripwire

- Three Blocks of Wood

- One Rectangular Piece of Wood

- Glue

- A Spear of some type

- Five Nails

Instructions

The spear trap is a little bit difficult to wrap your head around if you're not used to dealing with physics but essentially you want two blocks of wood pieces so that a single spear can fit on top of them and then you want a third block to raise those other two blocks off of the ground at a slight angle. Then you want to add in a bit of glue so that you can hold this together on the edge of the third block. Normally, this would end here but there are some additional improvements that you can make to this design because this would have hit just below the crotch area and wouldn't be very effective for anyone that's not traveling upstairs. To get a better angle, you need to use nails to prop up the wood so that it can be increased in its angle. By placing three of the five nails underneath the third block of wood, you effectively raise this up to at least a 90-degree angle. Make a notch in the back of the spear so that you can place the tripwire or fishing wire in the back of the spear. The last step is that you need to find somewhere where you can put a nail on one side while also putting a nail on the other side but the nail on the other side needs to be hidden out of the area of attack of your opponent. Tie the tripwire or fishing wire to the first of these two nails, bring it around to the back of the spear where it will fit in the notch, and then bring the final bit of the wire loosely over the second of the two nails. What this will do is it will allow you to run down the hallway and pull on this wire so that it launches the spear.

However, there's one final problem with this complicated design because if you hold the tripwire too high off the ground then the spear will not be propelled by the tripwire but instead, it will be shoved off the bricks and onto the floor in front of it. In order for the spear to fly at your opponent, you need to have the wire be exactly level to the final angle of the third block. This will provide enough resistance so that the spear continues to go forward as it slides along these two other pieces of wood and ensures the level of the tripwire isn't high enough to where it begins to push the spear downwards and the spear will release once the tripwire is no longer attached to it. Additionally, you want to make sure that the spear is placed really far back and that the tip of the spear is vertically aligned with the third block so that you get the maximum amount of pull on that tripwire whenever you activate it.

Chapter 3 – Nail Traps

Nail In Wood

Items

- A Nail

- A Rectangle Piece of Wood

Instructions

If you want a really cheap form of a Caltrop than this is the section for you because all you need to do is hammer a nail into a piece of wood and just make sure that the point is sticking up. These small things are extremely easy to make and will be sustainable once we run out of factories that produce flat wood and nails and they do a lot of damage. You can not only stick them underneath rugs, you can also hide them in the grass out in the yard. It's a wonderful little device that will do a lot of damage to your opponent's foot or even paws.

Hidden Rake With Nails

Items

- Rake

- Nails

- Glue or Hammer

Instructions

If you ever watch cartoons then you will have seen the moment where the character steps on the rake and manages to smack himself in the face with a rake handle. This is actually the same thing that happens in real life and I can attest to walking on a rake and whacking myself in at least the body but not the head because the rake itself is rather dull so it doesn't really damage the foot unless it's sharpened whereas the rake is also built so that if you do step on it, it bends forward on its curved access and the wood does come up. This makes this cheap tool a very good ready-made trap for those who are trying to make a good defense for their home. The ideal spot for this is tall grass because you don't want your opponent to see that you have this but sometimes you can put it in the dark and it'll do just as much damage. Essentially, you either want to nail the nails into the top handle of the rake or you want to move them on top of the rake and gluing them is often more damaging than nailing them into the handle because the glue allows for the nails to come off and stay inside of whatever they punctured.

A Bed of Nails

Items

- Small Nails

- Glue

- Thick Carpet

Instructions

This is a more sneaky way of protecting your house but essentially you want a very thick carpet that is malleable in that it's fluffy or has a lot of cushion to it rather than its thick because it's been threaded thick. Then you want to flip it over to the bottom and poke the nails through that you want inside of the carpet and these can either be small nails or larger nails, but the smaller the nail the easier it is the height. The reason why you might want bigger nails is because bigger nails will do much more damage than the smaller nails. In order to keep these in place when you put the carpet down and when you bring the carpet up, you generally want to apply a copious amount of glue to the sections you poke through. This will prevent the nail from losing its place inside the carpet so long as you don't handle it roughly. All you have to do in order to use this is put it in front of a door or an area where you think they might be walking through and they open the door only to find that when they step down their foot is full of nails.

Nail swing set

Items

- Linked Nails (They can come like this but you can also just tie nails side by side)

- Tripwire

Instructions

This trap is rather cruel in its design because it allows you to just impale your opponent before they ever get to you but I want to stress that you need to be very careful with this type of trap because it could easily turn against you. The idea is that you have a long link of nails that can be swung from the ceiling at your discretion. Therefore, all you have to do is use three nails so that you can first hang the linked wires up by the tripwire and then place the third nail for you to hang the other nails on. If you want to set this up so that a person has to activate it rather than you reaching up and letting it slide down then you could easily put a piece of tripwire down by their feet and bring it up towards the middle of the link chain where you'll be resting the chain against the third nail in the ceiling. By doing this, you essentially create a trap where they pull on the tripwire and this pulls the linked nails down so that it goes below the nail that they're resting on and swings at your opponent with full force. Again, this is a very nasty one that could easily turn on you if you don't put it in the correct area or if you accidentally hit the tripwire without meaning to because once it's flying you can't exactly stop it.

Chapter 4 – Physics Traps

Jax of Wood and Sap

Items

- Sap or Glue (Sap if you're out in the wild)

- Sharp Wood

- Shovel

Instructions

I just want to be clear about this trap because this trap can actually be made of nails instead of wood but if you want to make some type of trap in the future that is made of wood because you have no nails then you can use this type of trap. Essentially, all you want to do is connect the sharp bits of wood so that they are pointing in every different direction and then you want to cover them with sap or glue and let them dry. The reason why this is a physics trap is because whenever somebody stands on this, while some parts may actually be pushed down and not puncture the skin some of the other parts will find resistance and the moment they find resistance the wood becomes a solid object that cannot be pressured to go downwards with a small amount of force and that will be the wood that punctures the skin.

Hidden Rake With Wood

Items

- Rake

- Drill and drill bit

- Metal Cylinder the size of the drill bit

- Wood

- Glue

Instructions

If you are the type of individual that has a family and you're trying not to build traps that will kill your opponents because you worry about the fact that the same traps could result in the death of your family members, then a similar item to the hidden rake with nails is the hidden rake with wood. The difference between the two is that the nails are meant to permanently damage if not kill the opponent while the one with wood is meant to do damage but also not kill the opponent. All you want to do is drill a hole in the right side where you can slide the metal cylinder in and then apply glue to both sides of the cylinder. Then you want to drill another hole in a piece of wood and slide the cylinder through this hole so that the cylinder is connected to both the rake and the wood. Allow this to solidify and just hide it somewhere. Ideally, you want to choose a somewhat large block of wood but nothing that you couldn't easily pick up and throw. A large block of wood would do a lot of damage but if it's too heavy then your opponent will be able to stop it from coming out because all they have to do is simply stop applying force and the weight of the object will push it back down rather than carry it forward. This is an ideal trap for those who have family members that will be with them during these trying times. You don't really want to kill family members.

Swinging Portrait

Items

- Old Portrait Frames

- Wire

- Lots of nails

Instructions

The swinging portrait trap is actually really simplistic once you think about it because it often represents the swinging that you see in nearly every treasure adventure movie that's ever been made. The only difference is that portraits are known to be very heavy and cause a decent amount of damage but also rather cheap in their expenditure and they already have hooks for them to hang on. In order to make this, you first need to set up a number of portraits. Essentially, all you want to do is you want to put a row of nails in the ceiling and then tie wire to them and then tie that wire to the portraits. Then you want to run the wire through the empty holes of the portrait frames and attach that to something that your opponent can trip on before they get to the area where the portraits will swing. You can do this by putting a nail in the wall and loosely tying wire to it and then run that wire to another nail on the opposite side where it is again loosely tied, and then this can be run across the area where you plan for them to trip where you can securely tie it on the opposite end. Therefore, the opponent will walk through the tripwire and the wire will be pulled out so that it is no longer supporting the portrait frames and your opponent is now walking into the line of fire of several different portraits swinging back and forth. This is an excellent trap to not only do damage to your opponent but also slow them down because it will take them time to stop the portraits from moving because our natural reaction towards swinging objects that don't hurt us is to stop the swinging object before moving forward. This is especially true if the opponent is working with a team of people.

Classic Marbles

Items

- Marbles

Instructions

Even though the movies have probably beaten this one to death, one of the best ways to defend yourself while you're on the run is to throw a jar of marbles behind you so that it shatters and spreads the marbles over the floor. However, you don't want to throw the jar too hard because if you throw the jar too hard then the marbles will only stay in place for a short period of time. Instead, you want to throw the marbles behind you in a tossing not throwing fashion so that there's not much impact whenever it hits the floor but when it does it impact, the marbles fly out behind you. This further increases the chances that the opponent will trip on these marbles as they attempt to chase you. With this, you do need to make sure that the jar that you have is relatively thin so that it can be easily broken. While this may be one of the most overused stereotypical traps that you see in movies, this is a method that works very well and it has been proven that if you use this trick then your opponent is highly likely to trip and fall all over themselves. If you don't want to use marbles, you can always use something that is similar like Legos but they don't work as effectively as marbles since they are not usually spherical objects.

Conclusion

Welcome to the end of this book and while we've gone through a lot of different traps what you have to keep in mind is that you don't have to actually use all of these traps. The idea of a trap is not to create an Indiana Jones type maze in your house but rather to help secure areas where you wouldn't normally be able to protect them well. Unless you're an individual who is by yourself and you are just trying to survive by yourself, you most likely want to use some of these traps when you absolutely have to rather than on a daily basis because a lot of these traps do a lot of damage. You don't really want a 5 year old or 10 year old to be stepping on a ball of spikes created at home because not only is that a horrible experience for the child and yourself but it could also mean that you could easily not only lose the child but also end up in a mental facility because you were trying to do something good for the child but you ended up harming them. I don't see how protecting your child from the end of times by building a spike trap with glue and wood would really hold up in a court system without being called insanity. Sure, it makes sense to you and I because we are prepping for such times but to regular people, it just wouldn't seem quite what it is. In saying that, I do hope that you are very careful about which traps you choose to use and where you choose to use them so that you can not only better protect your family for the future but also protect your family for the here and now.

FREE Bonus Reminder

If you have not grabbed it yet, please go ahead and download your special bonus report *"DIY Projects. 13 Useful & Easy To Make DIY Projects To Save Money & Improve Your Home!"*

Simply Click the Button Below

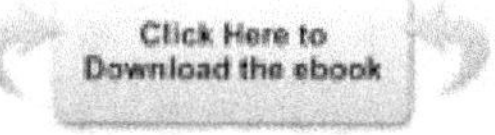

OR **Go to This Page**

http://diyhomecraft.com/free

BONUS #2: More Free & Discounted Books or Products

Do you want to receive more Free/Discounted Books or Products?

We have a mailing list where we send out our new Books or Products when they go free or with a discount on Amazon. Click on the link below to sign up for Free & Discount Book & Product Promotions.

=> Sign Up for Free & Discount Book & Product Promotions <=

OR Go to this URL